Hold Fast

A Devotional for Military Wives

Katie Windsor

Hold Fast

A Devotional for Military Wives

Katie Windsor

River Birch Press
Daphne, Alabama

Hold Fast: A Devotional for Military Wives
by Katie Windsor

Unless otherwise identified, Scripture is taken from the King James Version of the Bible in public domain.

ISBN 978-1-956365-52-8 (print)
ISBN 978-1-956365-53-5 (e-book)

For Worldwide Distribution
Printed in the U.S.A.

River Birch Press
P.O. Box 868, Daphne, AL 36526

To Jesus for giving me the words, wisdom,

strength, and courage in my marriage.

To my husband, Troy Ret. U.S.M.C Veteran,

who's given me the best marriage any wife

could ask for and for supporting me in this life.

To my children, Noah, Carly, Mark, Cass,

Madi, and Gracy for loving me, encouraging me, and

praying for me.

Contents

Preface *ix*

Introduction *xi*

1 Fighting the Real Enemy *1*

2 A Soft Answer *6*

3 Encourage Daily *12*

4 Love Passionately *15*

5 Being the Calm in the Storm *18*

6 Trusting in God Always *22*

Letter to a Military Wife *25*

Preface

Do you remember the day you met your husband? I sure remember the day I met mine. I have the most incredible man in my life. My husband strives to be a godly man in every aspect. However, having a mental illness due to the military has definitely been the driving force the devil uses to attack everyone outside his precious brain. Initially I said, "Yep, this is the one, this is the guy I'll spend the rest of my life with." We met online because that was the trend at the time. My husband, Troy, and I didn't date traditionally or biblically. We felt like marriage was just two people who live together yet do their own thing. It wasn't until after I'd been saved a few years and received countless hours of godly counsel and advice, that I realized there was so much more to being a wife and that there's even more to being a military wife.

Before we started dating, my dad, an Army veteran, warned me NOT to marry a Marine. I laughed it off until I saw what he was meaning. Military husbands are just different than civilian husbands. They've experienced things that nobody else has experienced or faced.

Within the first 6 months of dating, I saw things I'd never seen before except for a few traits I saw in my dad growing up. I saw things such as PTSD, anxiety, tremors, and many more neurological disorders. So began our journey together, and I wouldn't trade it for anything in the world.

Years later, I've had the joy of helping fellow Christian women who have military husbands. I have shared with them the godly counsel I have received along with scripture verses and life experiences in certain situations that our husbands face that a civilian husband may not encounter.

Whether your husband is on active duty, recently discharged, or is a 15+ year veteran, there's something in God's Word that still applies today. I wrote this devotional with y'all in mind! When God gave me a desire to help fellow Christian military wives find their way through a marriage that was meant just for them, I listened and obeyed.

My hope throughout this entire book is to help give wisdom, courage, hope, and comfort through my life's experiences thus far. This devotional is not a cure-all book nor will it give you superwife powers. Believe me, I tried.

Nevertheless, I do believe that you'll walk away with a better understanding of your husband and the day-to-day struggles he faces as well an encouragement to you as a wife that it will be worth it all.

Introduction

I am not perfect, my marriage is not perfect, my children are not perfect, but God is, and his Word is perfect. When moments of hardship, frustration, and conflict occur . . . when you feel like there's just no hope and you want to give up . . . when you feel like no matter what you do, say, or act, it's never going to be good enough . . . when you feel overwhelmed, exhausted, worried, or anxious . . . when you experience fear and doubt . . . know that I've felt all those things for many years before I made some changes in my life.

There are still moments that arise, but God's given me so much strength, wisdom, and courage to face anything that happens within my marriage.

For the next few chapters, I want to bring up some common topics that military wives face daily. As you read, please keep an open heart. Again, this is not a cure-all but a help-all if you will. My husband, Troy, and I have been married for fifteen years, and through these years, I've seen God's mighty hand over and over again.

One

Fighting the Real Enemy

Most of the time if I were to go to a sporting event, or the store, or basically anywhere else than my own home and I was cursed at, spoken ill of, or called every name under the sun, it would be pretty easy for me to just brush it off. If I don't know someone, nor do I really care to know them, their opinion would be irrelevant to me.

However, when I am spoken to unkindly, or perhaps with belittling statements, and it's coming from my husband, that's when I hurt the most, that's when I get offended the easiest, and that's when I want to retaliate.

Most military men have a sense of control that they want to keep. When that control is has gotten out of hand, even just slightly, irrational behavior can result. Life for X many years for them has been regimented, orderly, and just the perfect way it should be. But when you add simple civilian wives into the mix who either don't understand what they are communicating or maybe who don't think the same way, sometimes things don't turn out that great.

One of my biggest issues was watching my husband make decisions that I thought were either unwise, not correct, or could hurt the family. With some of it, I was right. What he was doing or about to do could impact our family in a negative way.

I wanted to prevent it, so I took matters into my own hands. I began nagging, telling him what to do, when to do it, and how to do it, thinking that was my best way of helping. You know what I found when I did that? More strife. We found ourselves fighting like cats and dogs daily over even the smallest things in the world. Our marriage was not very good. When I told him the "best" way to do something, I was verbally attacked in return every single time.

And what happens when I get verbally attacked? I get offended and hurt and want to make sure he knows just how hurt I am. What would that look like? Depended on the comeback from him, I'd either ignore him for a few days, have him make his own meals, or speak unkind words with an attitude. The worst part is that then I'd start making my own decisions, basically overstepping him. Not once during that whole time, did I stop and consider who I was really fighting against.

When we first got married, I knew my husband had some mental issues. One of them occurred when there was a set routine and then for some reason, something didn't happen the way he wanted it to or maybe the time changed. Immediately he would verbally attack me, for I must have been the one at fault. However, I honestly didn't care, and I figured he was handling it like a normal man. Then, when I saw that it was getting worse every time we were together, I just couldn't handle it much more I reached out to our pastor's wife. This woman not only was able to help me, but she began to shape me into the woman I am today. First thing is that she reminded me that there is a bigger enemy that we are fighting, and it was not necessarily my husband. Yes, these things were coming from my husband's lips or attitude, but there was a bigger enemy. It was the devil using my husband against me. She explained that who better to use against us than the ones we love the most to attack us. They are the ones who can unmistakingly shake us to the core.

Not long after our meetings, I was given a set of scripture verses to hide in my heart. For every moment that occurred when there was frustration or stress and the words spoken by my husband were out of frustration, I learned to:

1. Stop and consider who I was really fighting.

2. Bring that scripture to my mind to control my spirit before the situation is made worse. One of my favorite Bible verses for remembering that I am not fighting against my husband but, in fact, the devil is found in Ephesians 6:12.

   For we wrestle not against flesh and blood, but against principalities, against powers, against the rulers of the darkness of this world, against spiritual wickedness in high places.

So ladies, I'd like to share these scripture verses with you in hopes they will give you re-assurance and comfort, knowing that there's a bigger enemy that we are fighting and it's NOT your husband. Satan is using your husband against you in your moments of weakness. Using God's holy Word to battle Satan is the best way to communicate to your husband that you love him, you care about him, and you are there to support him even in the middle of a storm.

> *Be sober, be vigilant; because your adversary the devil, as a roaring lion, walketh about seeking whom he may devour* (1 Peter 5:8).

> *Submit yourselves therefore to. Resist the devil, and he will flee from you* (James 4:7).

> *The thief cometh not, but for to steal, and to kill, and to destroy* (John 10:10).

Neither give place to the devil (Ephesians 4:27).

Put on the whole armour of God, that ye may be able to stand against the wiles of the devil (Ephesians 6:11).

For we wrestle not against flesh and blood, but against principalities, against powers, against the rulers of the darkness of this world, against spiritual wickedness in high places (Ephesians 6:12).

Two

A Soft Answer

I grew up in a LOUD family. We talk loud, we cheer loud, we sing loud, and unfortunately we fight loud. My whole life I've only replied to what I felt was an attack against me with revenge in my speech, especially if you were going to accuse me or put the blame on me. I was gonna let you have it and make sure you know just how upset I was. I mean, hello. I don't deserve to be spoken to with unkindness or harshness, especially when someone is speaking lies against me. No way!

For the first five years of our marriage, there was no way I was going to let him "win" in any argument. I was going to make sure that he not only knew how hurt or upset I felt, but I was going to punish him for the way he spoke to me. My husband has never been physical with me or any of the kids, but he has always just been hurtful with his words.

You may be asking, how'd that work out for me? Well let's just say that we got nowhere every single time. I just spewed frustration, anger, and resentment, and it sure didn't help our kids any. I can still remember the day our pastor's wife approached to tell me that our children have been asking her to help us because all we ever did was fight.

That moment right there made me stop short in my tracks. I felt so ashamed, hearing that from her. I mean, I sort of knew the kids would hear us, we were loud enough, but I'd hoped that it wouldn't affect them. I was wrong, and I needed to hear that from our pastor's wife. I made the decision right then and there to make a change. How could I do it, though, when I felt so hurt and embarrassed, and it was just so frustrating? That's when the following verse was given to me. This verse has truly became my life verse.

> *A soft answer turneth away wrath but grievous words stir up strife* (Proverbs 15:1).

Let's just take a moment and pick this verse apart. A soft answer turns away wrath. What does it mean to have a soft answer? I wondered if perhaps that means I should speak in a calm tone in return? When my husband and I were in a strong disagreement about homeschooling, for example, I believed they needed to be homeschooled, and my husband just couldn't handle the idea. I wanted to win that fight with everything in me.

Then, I reminded myself that no matter what, my husband was the head of this family and that I should be happy and content with whatever decision he made, even if I felt it wasn't the correct decision. So, in the midst of us shouting and battling with words, I paused a moment, took a deep breath, let it out slowly, then responded with a calm tone and controlled breathing "I'm sorry. I just feel so strongly that this is what we should be doing; however, I will follow you in whatever decision you make." The whole situation deescalated almost immediately. We were able to communicate with love and kindness to each other within the next ten minutes and find middle ground.

Maybe having a soft answer means I don't respond cynically? It's so easy for me to not only point out my husband's flaws but remind him that he is so self-centered. In that moment, isn't being self-centered what I am doing? Am I choosing my own way and making sure that I am the one who wins a fight and gets their way? God wants us to be humble. God wants us to prefer the other person over ourselves all of the time. Our pastor made the following statement perfectly, and I've never forgotten it. "One decision makes them all." If I just decide to have a soft answer in times of chaos or frustration, it would not only make it easier for me to continue giving a soft answer, but it will also help my husband deescalate and be the man God wants him to be.

Lastly, not responding at all and just giving the situation time is sometimes the best answer you can give. My husband likes to speak out loud. Sometimes he does need help, and sometimes he speaks in frustration. I used to think by giving him help or advice in the midst of him reacting was the best thing I could do. I quickly found out that it made things worse. This was something that took me a long time to practice but learning to allow your husband to just vent, or grumble, or speak out loud is the very best thing.

One good example of that in my life was when my husband and I were in the middle of putting together furniture. It went something like this:

Husband: "UGH! I can't figure this out, it's just not working for me."

Me: Silence

Husband: "If only I could figure out if and how this piece will work."

Me: Silence

Husband: grumbling and mumbling

Me: Silence

Husband: "Okay, okay, I think I've got it. Hang on, lemme just . . ." (fixing the piece he needed to complete the project).

Me: Silence

Husband: "Whew, okay, there we go. Good job. (And he had a good spirit.)

Me: "You're so smart and so strong."

Husband: Smiles with confidence.

Plenty of times I don't say a word. Even when it seems like the situation is just in total chaos! I want to say something, even encouragement, but I know when I open my mouth it's gonna end up putting us in a worse situation than we were already in.

Ladies, having a soft answer will always be the right answer. Even when you give a soft answer, and there's still contention and rude responses, believe me, having a soft answer will always be the right answer. Here are some Bible verses that help us to remember that we must have a soft answer when speaking to our husbands.

A soft answer turneth away wrath, but grievous words stir up strife (Proverbs 15:1).

Answer not a fool according to his folly; lest thou also be like unto him (Proverbs 26:4).

She openeth her mouth with wisdom; and in her tongue is the law of kindness (Proverbs 31:26).

Let no corrupt communication proceed out of your mouth, but that which is good to the use of edifying, that it may minister grace unto the hearers (Ephesians 4:29).

Three

Encourage Daily

I am not sure about anyone else, but I love to be encouraged. Even better, I love encouraging others. Now, my husband is a Marine, which means he's trained himself to just eat, sleep, survive, repeat, mentally of course. So, when he is not having the greatest day, he still just pushes through. There's a very sedative expression on his face. You could tell him the funniest joke on the planet and receive nothing in response. Sometimes, there's even a sarcastic response.

What do I do in this situation? First, I always stop and pray for him, for his heart, and for whatever it is that he is struggling with. Then, I encourage! There's so many different ways in which you can be a daily encourager to your husband. Here's just a few that have worked for me:

Verbally encourage—Tell him how handsome he

looks today. Tell him how proud you are of . . . (whatever you are proud of that he's done.) Tell him that you think he is wise and so deserving of . . . (whatever you believe).

Give him gifts—these can be whatever your heart desires. If you are a crafty woman, make him something. If you enjoy baking, bake him something JUST FOR HIM! Perhaps you're at the store. Purposely look for something that would brighten his day. Give him some cash and tell him to just go get something he wants. Make something specialized or custom made for him online.

Write him notes—I have purchased small sticky notes and placed them EVERYWHERE he goes—in his truck, on the mirror in the bathroom, on the fridge. Anywhere! Write him a letter on nice paper and spray it with your perfume. Send him text messages to let him know you are praying for him and love him. Then, stop and pray for him.

Not every time will this be a fix-all, but I guarantee you that when you become your husband's biggest encourager, he will feel so much more important, and in the end, it will truly help him spiritually.

Here are some verses of encouragement that I have found help me before I try to help him with encouragement:

Every word of God is pure: he is a shield unto them that put thier trust in him (Proverbs 30:5).

I can do all things through Christ which strengtheneth me (Philippians 4:13).

Now the God of hope fill you with all joy and peace in believing, that ye may abound in hope, through the power of the Holy Ghost (Romans 15:13).

Cast thy burden upon the Lord, and he shall sustain thee; he shall never suffer the righteous to be moved (Psalms 55:22).

Rejoicing in hope; patient in tribulation; continuing instant in prayer (Romans 12:12).

For I know the thoughts that i think toward you, saith the Lord, thoughts of peace, and not of evil, to give you an expected end (Jeremiah 29:11).

Be strong and og a good courage, fear not, nor be afraid of them; for the Lord thy God, he it is that doth go with thee: he will not fail thee, nor forsake thee (Deuteronomy 31:6).

Four

Love Passionately

When I first met my husband, all I ever wanted to do was to sit and kiss him and be with him physically. I am pretty biased, but he is the sexiest man I've ever seen in my own opinion.

There's a struggle that every man faces with his flesh. Military men, many times, have a past. In my husband's case, there were quite a few party nights while he was in the military. I met him seven years after he was discharged.

I always wanted to make sure that I was the one who was loving him passionately and the one woman that he thinks about daily, not even giving him a chance to think of anyone else. What does this look like? Just a few things that I've decided to do that's helped our marriage.

1. I enjoy hearing him talk about his military life—the job he had and the events that occurred during his time in the military. However, I know that when he reminisced on those times, there was a past connected to them, typically dealing with girls they would party with. So, I recreated the events in his mind of what would have happened if it was me instead.

2. I text him daily with flirtatious talk, making him want to be around me every minute he gets. I'll text him enticing thoughts of what we could be doing instead of work.

3. I'll send him pictures—not pictures that would get you in trouble but rather something just enough to get him thinking about you.

4. When he comes home, I greet him with a passionate kiss, touching him passionately. As wives, we are commanded to love passionately even if our husbands have had a bad day or are in a bad mood. Learn the balance. For my husband, when he is just not having a good day then I won't "love" passionately, but instead I will walk by and touch him occasionally just to let him know what I'm thinking.

God's Word has helped me in remembering that no matter how the day has been. I need to be there sexually for my husband as well as making myself available for him any of the time.

> *By night on my bed I sought him whom my soul loveth* (Song of Solomon 3:1).
>
> *His left hand should be under my head, and his right hand should embrace me* (Song of Solomon 8:3).
>
> *Therefore shall a man leave his father and his mother, and shall cleave unto his wife: and they shall be one flesh* (Genesis 2:24).
>
> *Let him kiss me with the kisses of his mouth: for thy love is better than wine. Because of the savour of thy good ointments thy name is as ointment poured forth, therefore do the virgins love thee. Draw me, we will run after thee: the king hath brought me into his chambers: we will be glad and rejoice in thee, we will remember thy love more than wine: the upright love thee* (Song of Solomon 1:2-4).
>
> *Marriage is honorable in all, and the bed undefiled* (Hebrews 13:4).

FIVE

Being the Calm in the Storm

Military men already have so much going on inside of them. Whether it's physical, mental, or medical, they are fighting a battle that no civilian man could understand. Then, add the daily life schedule on top of it and then a marriage and children. There's nearly a constant storm brewing inside of your military husband, but you can become the calm in his storm. I know, sometimes this seems nearly impossible.

My husband suffers from tremors, anxiety, and PTSD. When moments arise, he loses control. He begins to shake furiously, his speech becomes impaired, he can't focus, and then it's just downhill from there until it subsides. Most of the time he gets this way when frustration strikes. It's kind of like being at the airport for five hours, finally boarding a plane, getting settled, and then being told to deboard the plane and find another flight. You learn that the soonest flight would be at midnight, and then you have to rent a car from a different city and drive the remainder of your trip.

For years when moments like this have occurred, I start to see the green monster emerge. I thought the best thing for me to do is "fight" him in return and show him how silly he was acting. I then learned very quickly that didn't work. So, after seeking counsel, I realized that just holding his hand, maybe touching his back, and then sitting back and allowing him to go through this episode.

Jesus is our calm in the midst of the storm. When we, as military wives, decide to be the calm for our husbands, this tends to help deescalate the situation. Perhaps your husband just received a text message from a wayward child, and it's just too much to bear. Taking his hand, holding him tight, and letting him know you are BY HIS SIDE may be the absolute best thing to do!

The doctor's office may call and give him some pretty grim news that although you may be able to beat it, it's going to be a trial. Just sitting beside him assures him that you aren't going anywhere.

Or maybe he's having flashbacks again with night sweats, screams, uncontrollable shaking, verbal attacks, and panic. Don't leave his side. Stand by him, sit with him, and comfort him. Be there for him. It doesn't matter how tough your husband is. He needs his wife to be the calm in the middle of that trial. When Job lost everything he had, his livestock, his possessions, his children, and then became ill, what did his wife do? She told him to curse God and die. As wives we don't want to be like Job's wife. We want to be the wife that assures our husbands that everything going to be okay and that we are not going anywhere. We will stand beside him through it all.

During the first five years of our marriage, I can tell you our life wasn't pretty. When he'd get frustrated, I'd either get frustrated as well and turn into a Karen, or I'd try to fight against him and paint him as a bad person to others because of his irrational actions.

An incident happened two years ago when we were at the airport. We knew there was a high possibility that things were not going to go the way that we wanted them to go. Sure enough, things escalated quickly with all the passengers but especially with my husband. At first, I grabbed his hand and just held on tight. Then, I started to touch his back softly. Finally, I whispered to him, "It's okay, I'm totally glad we get to spend any time together regardless of where we are at. Would you like me to get you something to drink?"

Almost immediately I saw him start to relax and unclinch his hands. Although he was still frustrated, he wasn't nearly at the level where he started, and that was the goal. Learn your husband and see what works best for him, whether it's food and drinks, soft music, just holding him. The time to talk to your husband of course is NOT in the middle of a battle but rather on a regular day. Just sit with him and ask him what calms him down. Then, ask God to give you the strength to be the calm in your husband's storm.

These Bible verses I have found to help me stay and be the calm amid my husband's storms. I hope that you find them to be useful as well.

> *But I say unto you, love your enemies, bless them that curse you, do good to them that hate you, and pray for them which despitefully use you, and persecute you* (Matthew 5:44).
>
> *Jesus saith unto him, I am the way, the truth, and the life: no man cometh unto the Father, but by me* (John 14:6).
>
> *He hath made every thing beautiful in his time: also he hath set the world in thier heart, so that no man can find out the work that God maketh from the beginning to the end* (Ecclesiastes 3:11).

Six

Trusting in God Always

After I got saved, I "knew" I should trust God with my marriage, but I never did. It was as if I was always telling God, "You can't do this on your own." It was as if God didn't understand just how much pain and hurt I was feeling. I truly felt like God didn't understand what I was going through during the times that seemed unbearable, unfair, and just hurtful. How on earth could God understand?

I was quickly reminded by my best friend the story of Jesus on the cross, or even before the cross when people spat in his face, didn't believe he was who he said he was, and took on physical and mental abuse for our sins. God understands everything that we go through. Yet, he NEVER gives us more than what we can handle.

When I met my husband, I knew that there'd be

some hurdles and struggles along the way with his military past and his current neurological issues. I knew that God sent me my husband because he needed me and I needed him.

After experiencing nearly seven years worth of fighting, arguing, complaining, and at one point nearly giving up and walking out, I was told to give it to God and trust him. One of the absolute hardest things I've ever had to do is to trust God one hundred percent because we are so used to doing things ourselves, or at least we feel like we are the ones in control.

One particular incident is what made me believe and trust God with everything I have. My husband had been making irrational decisions for weeks. Most of these decisions were affecting the kids, and I just couldn't handle it anymore. So I began fighting back, trying to make my husband change based upon my words only, but things were getting so much worse.

I walked into my closet. Shut the door. Broke down and just called out to God. I poured my heart out to him. Within two or three days it was like a light switch flipped, and there was no more strife, he had completely changed his mind on this particular decision and I just stood in awe! My best friend told me to start praising God and that's just what I did. Remember ladies, God's in control of everything. He is in control of your next breath, what happens in your day, and he is in control of your husband, not you!

I remind myself so often of this truth because just when I feel like taking control, or when I feel like controlling my husband's decisions, I remind myself that God's the One in control! Here are some reminders that we can trust God with all our hearts.

> *What time I am afraid, I will trust thee* (Psalms 56:3).
>
> *It is better to trust in the Lord than to put confidence in princes* (Psalms 118:9).
>
> *In God have I put my trust: I will not be afraid what man can do unto me* (Psalms 56:11).
>
> *O keep my soul, and deliverer me and let me not be ashamed; for I put my trust in thee* (Psalms 25:20).
>
> *Trust in the Lord with all thine heart; and lean not unto thine own understanding (*Proverbs 3:5).
>
> *Trust in him at all times; ye people, pour out your heart before him: God is a refuge for us. Se-lah* (Psalms 62:8).
>
> *O my God, I trust in thee: let me not be ashamed, let not mine enemies triumph over me* (Psalms 25:2).

Dear Fellow Military Wife,

If you are reading this and you've never accepted Jesus Christ as your personal Lord and Saviour, let me plead with you today. Don't let another day pass without accepting Jesus' personal free gift of salvation. If you've read this and are still unsure where your future lies, then please let me help you. You don't need to speak it out loud but once you've accepted Christ, I guarantee you that he'll change your life forever, and you'll never feel ashamed again. Just repeat after me:

> Dear Lord, I come to you in prayer asking for the forgiveness of my sins. I confess with my mouth and believe with my heart that Jesus is your Son, and that he died on the cross that I might be forgiven. Lord, I believe that Jesus rose from the dead and I ask you right now to come in to my heart as my Lord and Savior. Amen!

Dear fellow sister, if you've prayed and accepted Christ in your heart, I am rejoicing with you. Allow Jesus to work in your heart, in your marriage, and in your family. I will pray for all of those who read this book and apply it to their lives.

Now, go and be the best military wife God's made you to be!

About the Author

KATIE WINDSOR is a Texas native who grew up in Oregon. She's been married to her Marine Corps veteran husband, Troy, for fifteen years. Together they have six children and three grandchildren. Besides her passion for writing, Katie enjoys helping military wives experience their true potential through Christ. She also enjoys trying to out- fish her husband during their free time.

Notes

Notes

Notes

Notes

Notes

Notes

Notes

www.ingramcontent.com/pod-product-compliance
Lightning Source LLC
Chambersburg PA
CBHW061327120626
46546CB00007B/2704
9781956365528